Svalbard

The land beyond the Northcape

***

Stefan Lundgren & Olle Carlsson

*S*valbard is an isolated place, so harsh and forbidding that it remained uninhabited by man virtually up to our own century. During four months of a never setting sun the frozen expanses around the archipelago are miraculously transformed into one of the most productive waters in the world. Waters nourishing mighty populations of seabirds and seals. Waters still supporting groups of whales. Waters along the frozen fringes of which the polar bear roams in search of prey. Set in these waters, like a pearl marbled in the black, red and brown of rock and the blue and white of snow and ice, majestically floating in the light of the midnight sun, you find this wilderness area of outstanding beauty.

We dedicate this book to Dennis Puleston, Master naturalist, artist, cofounder of Environmrental Defense Fund, who has deepened the understanding of Nature and its echosystems for countless people.

"SVALBARDR FUNDI"– SVALBARD FOUND

THIS VERY SHORT NOTE in the 1194 Icelandic Annals pinpoints the first known sighting ever of the archipelago between 10° and 34° East: 74° and 81° North in the Arctic Ocean. Situated half-way between Norway and the North Pole, this land, the size of the republic of Ireland, is a mere 600 miles from the Pole. The Norse word "Svalbard" means "cold coast," an apt name for a land which today is 60 percent covered by ice. So Norse sailors knew of it, but this knowledge faded away. In 1596 the Dutch seafarer Willem Barents rediscovered the land, and named it Spitsbergen, "The peaked mountains". Today this name is confined to the largest island in the archipelago, since 1925 a part of the Kingdom of Norway.

We, the compilers of this book, have both during several seasons returned to Svalbard in July and August, having had the fortune and joy to work there as zodiac drivers and naturalists. A deep engagement in this wilderness area has followed the love-at-first-sight. To be allowed to produce this book is therefore a privilege, and it is also something that we know that many co-travellers aboard the MS Polaris have been waiting for.

Stefan has joined the Polaris ever since her first cruise from the Norwegian coast to Svalbard in 1985. Olle has worked there for four seasons. We have been offered quite unique possibilities to document in notes and photographs the environment and its wildlife. The collection of fine photos Stefan has built up over the years has been presented in the lounge of the ship. The response to these slide-shows, as well as the express wish of many passengers, have convinced us that we should give our impressions a more permanent presentation. It is our hope that these pictures, notes and reflections will light the memories that those of you who joined cruises there brought home. Hopefully it will inspire more people to follow us to this miniature Arctic. It offers in concentration an abundance of Polar features in a geographically limited area, much of which is possible to cover in an expedition cruise, where the Polaris explores the rugged coastline and the spectacular, ice littered fjords.

A condition for obtaining these photos and close, lasting impressions has in fact been the Polaris. A nimble little ship with a shallow hull, she can – under the skillful navigation of experienced officers – take us all the way up to the tickling mustaches of the bearded seal, within smelling distance of the walruses or directly up to the curious look in the young Polar bear's eye. Or, for that matter, to a safe anchorage in a minor bay for an excursion on the tundra. And where conditions do not allow her to go, our fleet of inflatable zodiacs will take us.

The Polaris is a special ship, dedicated to the spirit of discovery. True as this is for her cruises in the Caribbean, the Amazon or the coasts of Europe – nowhere does it hold more true than in Boreal areas. Here ice – and weather conditions, in combination with a discovery-inclined staff and expedition leader, make every itinerary something to diverge from.

Since Sven Olof's Special Expeditions took care of the Polaris, she has truly gone through fantastic changes – and she ages in beauty. Every time we join her, we happily establish the fact that an enthusiastic crew has improved her, thus stressing the cozy atmosphere that always has been her hallmark. The natural history staff share and spread their knowledge in recaps and lectures, on the bridge and decks, making her an educational ship, a floating seminar. Rarely, do we think, have so many people had such a small ship to thank for so many revelations! And it is the passengers, not we, who coined the expression she is a "happy little ship." It is true, though, that all of us working on board are willing to subscribe to this .

The project has been made possible only through the favorable working conditions provided by the officers, crew and staff of the Polaris. We are two naturalists who compile these pages, but we feel part of a working team, where the contribution of each and every one on board is essential in making operations smooth and safe, and experiences truly rewarding.

Lund, Sweden, in June 1994

Stefan Lundgren & Olle Carlsson

FOREWORD

There are certain lands which inspire in certain people complete devotion. For Olle Carlsson and Stefan Lundgren, their devotion is for the high latitudes of Arctic.

For many years Olle and Stefan have spent a large part of their summers in Svalbard, great Arctic islands by the North Polar ice sheet. They have journeyed there aboard my ship, the M.S. Polaris, giving of their knowledge and enthusiasm to our guests.

Svalbard, for most of the year, is an impenetrable icescape, harsh beyond description. Yet, in the summer for a brief brilliant time, it comes alive. Wild flowers carpet the tundra, seabirds by the millions fish in the plankton-rich waters and walrus and Polar bear frolic on ice floes.

A year ago they suggested producing a book about this region and the voyages of Polaris. I knew that Olle was a really fine writer, and Stefan a poetic photographer. I was touched and agreed then and there to publish the book.

If you've visited Svalbard before, I hope you find this book a fitting tribute. If not, I hope it will inspire you to look north and discover for yourself the land of the ice bear.

Sven-Olof Lindblad

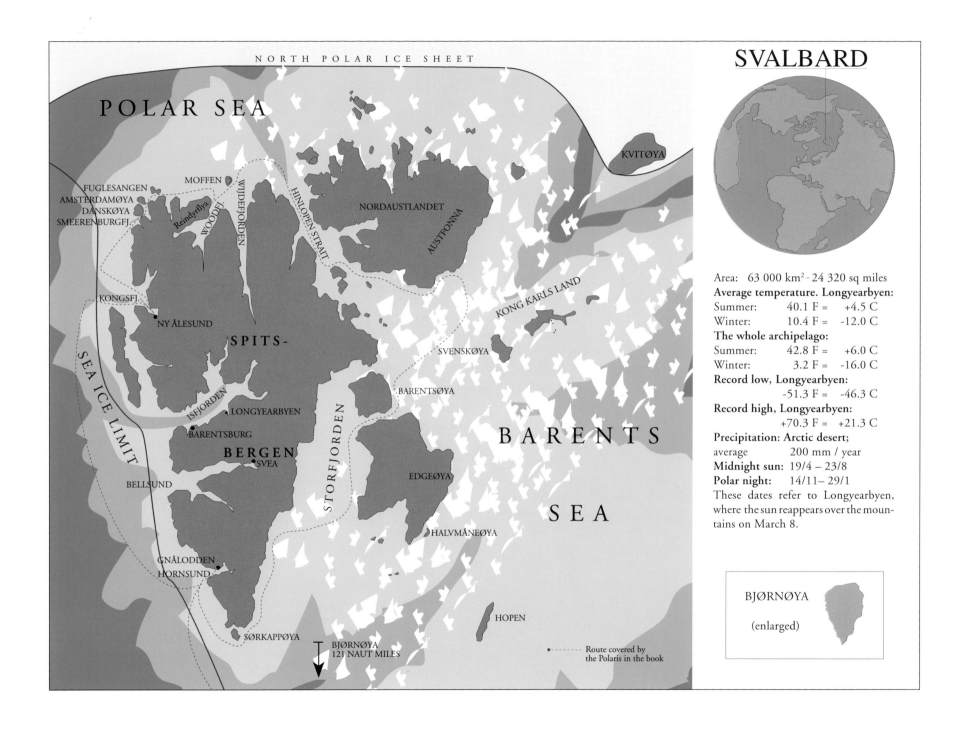

SVALBARD

NORTH POLAR ICE SHEET

POLAR SEA

KVITØYA

FUGLESANGEN
AMSTERDAMØYA
DANSKØYA
SMEERENBURGFJ.

MOFFEN

Reindyrflya

WOODFJ.

WIJDEFJORDEN

HINLOPEN STRAIT

NORDAUSTLANDET

AUSTFONNA

KONGSFJ.

NY ÅLESUND

SPITS-

KONG KARLS LAND

SVENSKØYA

SEA ICE LIMIT

ISFJORDEN

LONGYEARBYEN

BARENTSØYA

BARENTSBURG

BERGEN

SVEA

STORFJORDEN

BELLSUND

EDGEØYA

BARENTS

SEA

GNÅLODDEN
HORNSUND

HALVMÅNEØYA

HOPEN

SØRKAPPØYA

BJØRNØYA
121 NAUT MILES

•••• Route covered by
the Polaris in the book

Area: 63 000 km² - 24 320 sq miles
Average temperature. Longyearbyen:
Summer: 40.1 F =   +4.5 C
Winter: 10.4 F =   -12.0 C
The whole archipelago:
Summer: 42.8 F =   +6.0 C
Winter: 3.2 F =   -16.0 C
Record low, Longyearbyen:
               -51.3 F =   -46.3 C
Record high, Longyearbyen:
               +70.3 F =   +21.3 C
Precipitation: Arctic desert;
average   200 mm / year
Midnight sun: 19/4 – 23/8
Polar night: 14/11– 29/1
These dates refer to Longyearbyen,
where the sun reappears over the moun-
tains on March 8.

BJØRNØYA

(enlarged)

NORWAY – LAND OF THE MIDNIGHT SUN

Most expeditions to Svalbard, be they hunting or fishing expeditions, scientific ones or expedition cruises, traditionally have their starting point in Norway. The M S Polaris often launches her northbound journeys from here too, weaving her way through the archipelago off the Norwegian coast.

Like a floating needle on emerald velvet, deep down in the glacier carved valleys, she pierces the long narrow fjords, spreading a white lace of foam that slowly dissolves in her wake. On deck we tilt our heads back to marvel at the veils of the waterfalls washing the rock face. A couple of old farms nailed precariously to a mountain slope test our power to imagine what life must have been like up there

– The children were tied to the wall of the house when outdoors, the Norwegian pilot informs us on the bridge. He knows the places, having worked his way up and down the ship lanes for 20 years. Most of all these sights tell me the story of recent poverty in a land of mountains and fjord-infested coastline.

We leave our ship to zodiac-cruise some of the islands in this immense archipelago, like Reine in Lofoten – islands with small fishing villages embraced by steep mountains that lose their peaks in low-flying clouds and swirling swarms of seabirds.

These islands are also embraced by the Gulf Stream, which mitigates the colder coastal water into the right temperatures for spawning fish. All along, the fishing villages are constant reminders of Norway's traditional deep dependence on the sea; as far back as the Viking era, the bulk of the trade consisted of dried fish. Having faced over-fishing and depletion of the stocks of herring, cod and capelin, the backbone of the economy has switched to oil, a non-renewable resource of the sea that guarantees the country one of the highest standards of living in the world.

From the deck of the ship we enjoy a close encounter with a family of killer whales, or orcas, evidently a local pod with roots in Vestfjorden. They are feeding, flinging their powerful bodies through the water in a turmoil of splashes and whipped-up foam. A baby orca is hanging so close to her mother that it actually seems to be riding her back. Above the boiling water gulls flutter feverishly to take advantage of the confusion in the panicking school of prey. Says our geologist Jim Kelly on the bridge wing: "The herring are having a lousy day today!"

At 66° 33' North, just before midnight, we stop at the Arctic Circle and zodiac ashore on Vikingen, a small island crowned by a monument of the Globe, under which we congregate for the traditional toast of the warm, hot-spiced wine, Glögg, to celebrate the crossing. Our ceremony is noted by Ingeborg, the eternal sheep and the sole inhabitant of the island, relentlessly grazing its green slopes. No trace of emotion stirs her solemn face as she watches the sturdy tribe of Arctic plungers, a witless crowd of a dozen people who courageously submerge their bodies in the 50° F water. These brave ones are awarded a certificate to commemorate the deep chill.

We leave the majestic Norwegian mainland, worthy of a book of its own, under a sky of vibrating pale light. The further north we go, the higher the sun will spin across the sky, lighting the sceneries of the High Arctic.

66° 33' North. Vikingen. From now on the sun will no more dip under the horizon.

A DEAR CHILD HAS MANY NAMES

LEAVING TROMSØ, the city with the northernmost university and the most charming Polar museum in the world, we soon reach the last outpost of the mainland, Fugleøya. A sheer mountain rock breaching straight up from the depths of the sea, it is very worthy of its name, Bird Island. Here, swarms of puffins share real estate with the largest congregation in Europe of that impressive predator, the white-tailed sea eagle.

On sunlit days we have seen the puffins heading for the island and being sucked into the grassy slopes – vanished and gone! Only through binoculars can we see pinhead, white dots in the grass: the small birds at the entrance of their burrows, which they dig out in the soft ground with their colorful beaks, each couple creating a nest chamber for their single egg.

Puffins are a curious mixture of the solemn and the comical. But then again, as the French philosopher Henri Bergson has pointed out, "We can only laugh at an animal if it reminds us of a human being, if in it we find a human attitude or a human expression."

Their Latin name *Fracticula Arctica* translates "little brother of the Arctic," but they have many other names: the sea clown or the sea parrot – early whalers even discussed the "underwater parrot" they had seen. The English referred to it as the pope, while Icelanders were content with calling it the priest. A dear child has many names.

Above the puffins, on motionless wings fixed to the sky, soars the broad cross of the sea eagle. On a calm day we followed one of them spiralling from water level upwards on its nine foot motionless wingspan, all the way to the top of the cliff, on seemingly no wind at all. Enthusiastic shouts count the abundance of eagles:

– Five! There is another one emerging...no, two! – And there! Another three! They seem to be courting in the air!

Once, in 1989, this bidding in the feverish atmosphere of an auction, didn't stop until we had reached 24.

Apart from being a wildlife highlight, Fogleøya is the point at which most of us start to wonder – or worry – about the approaching sea leg to Bjørnøya, Bear Island. Ahead of us lie 240 nautical miles of exposed sea, affected by whatever winds that choose to sweep the water. And we know that the weather is very local and changes with no notice at all. Though usually quite calm, one memorable crossing made all our worst worries come true. Having checked with the weather stations at Bjørnøya and Tromsø we prepared for a pleasant crossing: calm weather, smooth seas were promised. Soon we found ourselves in a force 9 – 10 gale, pitching and rolling through fumes of salty spray under torn, overcast skies. Calling back to the station in Tromsø we found them more than reluctant to receive our corrections:

– No, no! We have checked with Bjørnøya. The weather is fine!

Drooping, silvery moustaches framing a melancholy face: The little brother of the Arctic, recorded to dive 250 feet in pursuit of small fish.

POLARIS' CROSSING

SETTING OFF FOR Bjørnøya we head parallel to the imaginary boundary where the Barents Sea meets the Atlantic water of the Norwegian Sea. To starboard the shallow expanse of the Barents Sea basin stretches all the way to Novaya Zemlya. More often than not the sea is calm at this time of year and so, pushed by gentle swell, the Polaris steams ahead, dragging in her wake flocks of soaring fulmars and kittiwakes. The sea itself rewards patience only. Shielding its secret inner life from our curious eyes, we can only calmly linger on the bridge and the decks, hoping for a moment of uncovering. And we are in good faith.

As usual, the crossing is filled to the brim with lectures by the naturalists and historians. Here is a chance to present important information on the areas we are heading for without being interrupted by landings, beautiful scenery or ... An outbreak from our biologist Art Cooley, dancing the ritual spotting-dance on sky deck, brings a stream of people from the lounge out on deck: "Dolphins to starboard!" In the midst of a lecture on seabirds a couple of smaller schools of the white-beaked dolphins are migrating through the water out there, their wet dark skin gleaming in reflected light.

A group of five suddenly turn and speed up, porpoising towards us for a joyful moment of bow riding. Hanging on the rail we watch them effortlessly glide at great speed on the pressure wave created by the ship, their white beaks clearly visible and their faint blows audible as they surface to exhale. Their flippers and flukes trail white slings of bubbles as they dance sideways to and fro, making visible to our eyes the transparent flow of water they are riding on.

Melville, renowned author of Moby Dick and a man with a great intuitional understanding of whales, once wrote: "When a man is tired of seeing dolphins at play, he is tired of life." What can we do but nod affirmatively to this statement each time the sea offers us the gift of a dolphin encounter? As suddenly as they appeared, they break away from the bow, speeding towards the horizon to join the porpoising dance of their school.

THAR SHE BLOWS

———◦———

THESE DOLPHIN-RICH waters were once also rich in whales. A merciless and profitable killing on a grand scale started around 1610, only years after Willem Barents' discovery. The seasonal hunting expeditions, engaging up to 12,000 people, mainly from England and Holland, were aimed mostly at Svalbard itself, but under way the waters around Bjørnøya also were emptied of their stocks of the great whales. Rarely do we see but the smaller minkies or – further north – belugas, in these waters.

With a cloud-covered Bjørnøya emerging on the horizon, almost everybody is already out on deck. There is not much wind to affect the blue water, not much wind to carry the shout of Tom O'Brian away:

– Thar she blows!

We respond with the second line of that old whaling song:

– Where she blows?

– At ten o'clock!

And to port we see the arched back and the dorsal fin of a minkie cleaving the surface. Most probably the whale is feeding, and the prey could be herring or capelin – being a baleen whale, it could even feed on shrimps, and the minkie is known to be an opportunist. This may sound bad, but in biological context, it just means that it feeds on what is available.

Tele-lenses appear en mass among the smaller automatic cameras along the rail as we wait for the next blow. This time the minkie exceeds our expectations – it actually heads for the Polaris, and soon blows close to port. As it slowly swims along the ship we get the best sightings you could ask for. With a final blow off the bow it disappears, accompanied by a sigh from one of the photographers on deck:

– First time ever I had too strong a lens on! Couldn't get the whole whale into the frame!

After the 1986 worldwide moratorium on whaling, scientific whaling has been pursued by Norway. In 1993 commercial whaling was resumed, in opposition to the decision taken by the International Whaling Commission. Norway has claimed it to be a democratic right for all countries to harvest their natural resources, as long as the species involved are not threatened. The minkie is no threatened species, and the initial quota of 290 whales is no doubt a sustainable yield. But there are many other aspects of whaling today. The international criticism has among other things pointed to the fact that whales migrate in and out of national water bodies, and that whaling, or the stopping of whaling, is an international responsibility.

The minkie, smallest among the baleen whales, and also the most abundant. Around 30 feet long, weighing 8 to 10 tons, it in the peak days of whaling was considered of no commercial interest.

BJØRNØYA – BEAR ISLAND

STANDING ALONE, close to the continental slope, Bjørnøya, at 74° 30' North, is but a rock cast in the sea. But geographically it is the southernmost outpost of Svalbard, in the winter embraced by pack ice. Roaming these enormous ice fields, the Polar bear at times makes land on the shores of the island, named for the first documented killing of one of these mammals in 1596. Bears are at times obviously more abundant than vegetation, and the only settlement, a small Norwegian weather station, boasts of having hosted the only carnivorous horse in the world. After the outbreak of World War II, the logistics of the island broke down, and being offered no hay the workhorse of the station turned to eating Polar bear meat!

A highly complex system of water bodies and currents, which extend into the whole of the Barents Sea, encircles Bear Island The most prominent feature is the meandering Polar Front. Here a branch of the Gulf Stream under much turbulence is forced down under colder, less saline Arctic water. Thus, and with the seasonal freezing and thawing of the sea surface, vertical movements are created which bring up minerals and nutrients for the algae. In the spring, when the sun throws her first blessing kisses on the ice cover, many of these algae begin to grow and bloom. On them an abundance of zoo plankton feed, turning the water into a nourishing soup for fish, seabirds and seals alike. In the sea lie the reasons for the teeming life around Svalbard and Bear Island, and the area may hold some of the densest bird populations in the world.

The Polar Front is not merely an immense food-producing feature.

Rarely is the word FOG spelled in larger capital letters than in the context of Bear Island. All seafarers that know the Arctic sea refer to it as Tåkeøya – Island of the Fog. During a couple of years in the late 19th century it was even known as The Kingdom of the Misty Island – at least by its self-proclaimed ruler, a weird German zoologist named Theodor Lerner, and his army of three. Lerner littered the place with claim posts stating "Private German property," but he disappeared mystically, leaving no trace of himself or his subordinates.

Seemingly, having adapted to the Polar night, the small hump of land avoids the scolding rays of the sun by being blanketed in fog most of the summer, fog simply produced in the mixing zone of the Polar Front, or by warmer air being blown in over the cold tundra ground. On clear summer days with outstanding visibility, the well-defined cloud of mist, like a fluffy cushion on the horizon, is what makes us understand that land is out there – hiding, but betrayed by what hides it. When all the sea was fog covered, the seafarers of the past were given the correct bearings for the island by the ever-increasing number of seabirds passing in the mist. The Polaris finds her way using more modern methods, and anchors in the sheltered natural harbor of Sørhamna. Standing at the damp rail we see silent, blurred silhouettes of birds threading their way through the mist. And we wonder at the small creatures' ability to find their specific ledge or burrow – guided by powerful, knife sharp senses of orientation in what, to us, appears to be a milky nothingness.

At the southern tip of Bear island: suddenly out of the mist and sea looms the Needle, a 240 feet solitary cliff, pointing like a finger to the sky.

TÅKEØYA – ISLAND OF THE FOG

THE WIND HAS RISEN, waves crimple the dark green water and the sheet of fog starts tearing apart and dispersing. Through holes and tunnels, beams of light pour down and move over the cliff-face in patches of melting gold and brown. Our zodiacs zoom in under the singing mountain, enveloped in the rank smell of guano and the high-pitched cries of tens of thousands of guillemots* and kittiwakes that cling to the ledges up there. Though every inch seems occupied, swarms of birds arrow through the air in all directions, making us wonder how they could possibly squeeze in. We are struck by the overwhelming amount of everyday bird life in this major metropolis. Some of us are hit by droppings as well, droppings that fall all around us, splashing the sea with pearly bands of sinking, recycled white nutrition. We drill our way through Pearly Gate, a long tunnel eroded right through the headline of the rock. Between the lips of a crevasse at the entrance, we spot the first downy kittiwake chick, and as we gush along the foot of the cliff, puffins and guillemots, rocking on the swell, fan away in a flurry of wings and paddling feet. With a stomach full of fish many plunge down under the surface, being unable to take off.

Today we enjoy row upon row of seabirds on Bjørnøya, nesting in overwhelming – but vulnerable – abundance. The depletion of populations of schooling fish by human fisheries also involves a price set on the puffins, the guillemots, on all the ocean birds – and on seals as well. The burden of starvation is theirs, leaving abandoned bird cliffs littered with the bodies of dead nestlings in its wake. In the years 1983–85 the capelin in the Barents Sea was heavily over-fished, and that triggered mass starvation among the adults of the most abundant species, the common guillemots. They decreased by 80 percent along the ledges of Bjørnøya in 1987.

We make a landing, usually at Walrus Bay – a name which today highlights the total absence of those mammals on the island. Instead the site is littered with decaying historical remains from the whaling and walrus hunting in the past.

"We had more than two hours to explore the rolling hills and to see much plant life that was new to us. There are at least seven species of saxifrage, including the beautiful purple species, Svalbard poppies were abundant, and on the higher slopes we found masses of the colorful roseroot with its rosettes of bright yellow and orange flower heads." *

And from here many prolong their walk and head for the bird covered cliffs along the trail marked out by the naturalists with small cairns – in case fog envelops you!

---

* In America called the muerre. Since Svalbard is part of Europe, we use the Brittish name.

* Log of Dennis Puleston, 1989

ACROSS TO SPITSBERGEN

DURING THE FOUR MONTHS of Polar night, the east side of the Svalbard archipelago freezes solid into the expanding Polar ice sheet. The west coast, being warmed by a tongue of the Gulf Stream, has to be content with being enclosed in drifting ice. When in July the Polaris glides into Svalbard waters, the west coast has long been ice-free – except for the times when the north-easterly Polar current pushes drift ice around the southern tip to surprise us.

In the comfortable warmth of the chartroom the Captain, officers and naturalists hang over the latest ice map, discussing the options. The east side is out of question this time, completely covered with dense pack ice, unbroken sea ice still plugging the Hinlopen strait to the north-east. Stefan is at his pessimistic very best, looking as if he has sudden blows of stomach pain adding to deep worries about the coming days: "This will be a very tough season. Maybe we won't be able to go to the really good places with all that ice." Captain Kent Grankvist gives him a cunning smile: "Keep that attitude up! It's the best guarantee for a successful cruise!"

We set course for the west side where no ice is shown on the map. But what about the low, illuminated part of the cloud-cover over the horizon? Could it be ice blink, light from the ice reflected on the clouds?

First strings of small ice lumps, like crushed meringue, meander on the swell. Then the ice grows ever denser, the floes bigger the further north we proceed. The swell dies out under the heavy lid of ice. We find ourselves zigzagging and pushing our way through an ice field reaching far out to sea off the south-west coast. Again the sea only rewards patience – maneuvering here is time consuming, but the beauty of the ever-changing ice that structures an otherwise rather monotonous sea is unsurpassable.

We stand on deck watching the stiff-winged fulmars tacking around the bow, sweeping the rails with their wing tips. Glaucous gulls appear as frost smoke rises in the cracks and leads between the ice floes. The strongly built predatory birds lower themselves on to humps on the floes, and in a stiff and solemn posture doing justice to their nickname "the mayor," they sternly watch the doings of the Polaris. Suddenly the sun breaks through and bathes the scene in a warm yellow light, in which the drift ice fades away into the foggy distance.

Hours still remain for us in the ice. We make slow progress towards the invisible land during the light night. To the North the cloud cover has lifted along the horizon, unveiling a sky of soft and mellow light. This is the end of the beginning of our journey; in the days and nights to come we will explore the coastal waters, fjords and inlets of Svalbard.

THE LONG JOURNEY

AT THE MOUTH OF HORNSUND, the southernmost of the great fjords, we anchor up. It is late evening, there is no wind. Some small snow flakes dance down and melt on the deck and rails. Most people on board have gone to sleep, rocked by the light swell that makes the Polaris chew her anchor chain like a horse chews his bridle. Over the waves we have reached our goal. Silence prevails, everything is at rest.

The Svalbard archipelago has undertaken an immensely long journey through time and space compared to ours to reach its present position. Starting in the vicinity of the equator the land mass has stubbornly headed north, driven by continental drift over the millions of years. It has been everything but a relaxed voyage: mountains have folded up and tumbled down, fissures and rifts have scarred the face of the land. Intrusive, molten minerals have forced their way into dormant bedrock, toasting and re crystallizing it.

Svalbard has been a shallow sea water basin where sand and clay turned into sedimentary bedrock. It turned into a coastal plain to rise again in folding and volcanic processes. At the latitude of present France it was a forested, lush green area housing the dinosaur Iganodon. Around the latitude of southern Norway, 50 million years ago, much of the vegetation was transformed into the heavy seams of coal that today are exploited by miners from Norway and Russia. Glaciers, rivers, heavy rains and frost, wind and heat have scraped, chiselled, tortured and sandpapered the bedrock. Thus remolded in the turmoil of periods of land building and eroding forces, it has shown an ever changing face to the world.

Much of the bedrock in Svalbard hides fossils, like petrified, scattered pages from a book on evolution. They cover most of the periods of the development of life on earth – from the earliest primitive fish and turtles to the first land living animals and the Iganodon. Being a land with very sparse, low-growing vegetation covering only 13 percent of the area, to the specialists it is like an open picture book on geological history.

At first we all wonder about the odd sceneries our geologist Ralph Hopkins directs his camera to, but we soon learn that here he finds the most exciting details revealing processes long gone. Enthusiastically he can document for future illustrated talks – or maybe a book? – on glacial and other features. And we are all very happy to help him:

– Ralph! Look at that neat brim line on the mountain slope, showing the level the scoring ice once reached. Wouldn't that be the perfect picture for page 27?!

AN ICE COVERED ARCHIPELAGO

ALL THE GEOLOGICAL FORMATIONS seem frozen, the archipelago seems to be resting in its final stage of transition. But heading into one of the Svalbard fjords, standing on deck in parkas and sunglasses, surrounded by the rocky shores where the gleaming glaciers wind down to the sea, we know that it is all going on right in front of us. The processes are most evident at the sites of retreating or advancing glaciers, where heavy walls of side and end moraines make up an easily readable text about never-ending erosion and deposition. We also know that the melt-water streams reposition silt, sand, gravel and stones: one stream in King's Bay alone has been measured to carry an average of 136 tons of eroded material a day throughout the summer! Evidence of this is the usually murky water that we glide through by the glacier fronts and far out in the fjords – though miscoloring at times is caused by plankton bloom rather than silt. Invisible to us is the still unbroken northward movement of the archipelago. Some calculations foresee it will reach the region east of the North Pole in 50 million years – much the way the Antarctic continent 50 million years ago glided into position over the South Pole.

Snow that falls in the interior of the Arctic desert of Svalbard accumulates to build up the ice sheets, which spread out into the spectacular glaciers that everywhere brighten our views of the land. They consist – like the toothed mountains they engulf – of a mineral: geologically, ice is a kind of a rock built of layers of never-melting snow. In the upper parts you can sometimes make out these layers of annual precipitation, like growth rings in a tree. They fade away further down, where the ice under the pressure of its own weight is re crystallized.

Ice holds many secrets and much information about ages past in its layered files; here you find trapped gases, wind-blown pollen, ashes from volcanic eruptions and airborne pollution. It offers knowledge about climatic periods and geological changes of the past, hereby handing down to us keys to the understanding of present and future processes like the global warming. Even more important is the way the ice deeply affects global everyday climate through its bare frozen existence, and how it "freezes" the seas at their present levels. If the ice in the world was to melt, the sea would rise by some 230 feet, giving the better part of humanity wet feet. In that perspective we all prefer minor, curious events – like ice spitting out a deep-frozen wandering salesman, in as perfect shape as his prehistoric clothes – the way it did in the Alps a couple of years ago!

What we see in Svalbard today are but small remains of the ice sheet from the last ice-age. Most of the glaciers are retreating and fading away, their withering tongues that once licked the sea suspended in their self-made U-shaped valleys. Usually the retreat is a slow process of much less than a foot a day. Advancing glaciers, though, sometimes let themselves loose in a galloping ice-surge. The stampeding flow of ice on one occasion advanced the Negri glacier in Svalbard at an average of 115 feet a day. When it came to a stop it had calved off 8 miles in one year!

The retreat of the ice also explains how at times we are able to bring the Polaris miles onto a glacier: we simply use a chart over 20 years old!

AN ICE LITTERED FJORD

In Smeerenburg fjord, we lower the zodiacs and cruise through the field of assorted ice, constantly fed by the calving ice wall. We pass sea birds decoratively positioned on chunks of ice, their own cruising vessels. We proceed slowly between ice-islets in layered shades of blue or embrowned by clay and sand, carrying large boulders of rock. The sun sparks flash in crystal clear ice, and a strong neon blue vibrates in cracks and holes of white icebergs. A couple of shining sculptures are a breathtakingly radiant blue: old, very dense and clean, ice from the bottom of the glacier. They would have made Henry Moore envious, and many of them trigger the flow of our imagination: an old dragon at rest, a lizard with paws outstretched, the bow of a sinking ship... And there are tunnels and holes to peer or photograph through. Stopping the engines we lean out and listen to the cracking and snapping sound of the ice as air bubbles burst out of their frozen prison. Once trapped by snow falling in the interior of the land and embedded in the scouring glacier, this air slowly descends to the sea and its release back to the atmosphere.

Ice, the frozen mineral, exhaling its lethal cold and killing life wherever it spreads, has always fascinated man – and always been feared by him. An obstacle that hinders seafarers, crushing ships or icing them down. A phenomenon holding more then 10 percent of the world in its frozen grip, the domains of which only a handful of sturdy animals have adapted to. Though dead, it is forever changing in front of our eyes, and thus gains the character of something living. Aesthetically one of the wonders of the world, we even perceive life in its dead body when talking about it as "calving".

We close in under the steep glacier, keeping a safe distance from its rugged and torn face. Only the humming of the outboard engine is heard as, in silence, we view the ghostly beauty of the ice-scape, leaning towers in all shades of blue, green and white, deep crevasses and fissures, caves and inlets, arches and protruding peninsulas of ice. Driven by tides and melt-water currents, the field of swimming ice is in constant unforeseeable motion, the turbulence in the murky water sweeping plankton and fish up to the surface. Along the foot of the ice wall concentrations of kittiwakes foam in feeding frenzy, and in and out of the deep blue of the ice caves they dart fearlessly. Still we see boulder-sized pieces falling from their ceilings or sliding down the front.

All of a sudden – a thundering, major outbreak! Tons of ice plunge into the sea, spouting and spraying water sky high. From a deep turbulence, waves rise and rush along the front and into the open water. With roaring engines we make our escape into the sheltering ice field, followed by a powerful swell that rocks and whips the floes. In a moment it is all over. Looking back we wonder: what can have happened to the bearded seal that we spotted swimming along the front seconds before the calving? Wouldn't there be casualties among animals taken by surprise at moments like this?

THE BEARDED SEAL – AND THE RINGED ONE

ICE ATTRACTS WILDLIFE: on the floes of glacial ice we usually encounter the bearded seals, resting, sleeping, drifting in the shallow waters of the fjords, dreaming bearded seals' dreams. Their small heads protrude from the blubbery sleeping bag of their body, which is of an impressive size; the biggest seals in the Arctic except the walrus, males and females alike are close to eight feet long, weighing at their best more than 600 pounds.

On a perfectly calm morning with excellent visibility our expedition leader Bud Lenhausen convokes the zodiacs over the radio. By the far end of the glacier he has spotted the oblong, cigar-shaped profile of a sleeping seal. She is a medium gray, the long hairs of her sensitive mustaches curled up – signs that she has been resting for a while in the sun, since right after feeding on bethnic creatures the whiskers hang down and the wet fur is a dark-brown tinge. Lying close to the edge of the floe, within easy reach of the safe escape into the water, she allows us to paddle all the way up to her before raising her head, giving us long thoughtful looks. Perhaps we are incorporated in and embroil her dreams: she seems a bit confused, even paralyzed, torn between wariness and curiosity. Like all bearded seals her face emanates a melancholy wisdom, which may reflect what one of the trappers in Svalbard told me: "Wisdom is necessary for animals that want to reach adulthood under the conditions offered in the Arctic." Having watched us for a while and concluded that we are no threat, she sighs, lowers her head to the ice and falls asleep again, the constant clicking of happy cameras sound-tracking her dreams.

It is as difficult to come close to the ringed seals, as it is easy to approach the bearded seal. Usually we see them early in the season, loosely scattered on rotting but still solid fjord ice. But this morning we enjoy a better encounter. Maybe the fact that we pop up surprisingly fast from behind an ice-sculpture is what gives a good viewing, maybe it is a young and naive seal. The silvery, spotted 165-pound mammal is the smallest and most abundant species in the Arctic, and thus a suitable prey for the Polar bear, to whom they are the favorite food and staple diet. Lying by breathing holes which they keep open with their claws in ice up to six feet thick, they make a very alert, not to say nervous, impression. They alternate second-long naps and swift checks of the surroundings, constantly fearing attacks from their enemy. That might also partly be the reason for the elaborate snow-cave the females build on the fast sea-ice. Here they give birth where they and their pups are out of sight. But not out of smell; even through a three feet thick ceiling, a bear can smell their presence from miles away and crash in. And an even more delicate problem the males must have during the mating season, when they declare themselves ready to mate by a strong smell…

With his head lifted, the front part of the body heaved up on stretched out flippers, the seal watches us, maybe wondering about our zodiac – a black ice floe of strange construction! Stiff and alert, in a frozen posture he waits for another move from us. And only fractions of a second later he has soundlessly slipped down his breathing-hole in the huge ice floe. Moments later an all white bird swings past us and lands on a nearby chunk of ice. The ivory gull, a high Arctic bird confined to these latitudes all year round, high on the list of every bird lover, highlights our morning. Remarkably, this little white beauty is very dependent on the ringed seal, in the winter predominantly feeding on the remains of blubber and flesh that Polar bears leave behind.

Following pages: the melancholly look of the bearded seal, the alert ringed seal, kittywakes resting on the ice and the all white ivory gull, the peace-dove of the Arctic.

THE HIGH ARCTIC STARTING RAMP

CRUISING THROUGH SØRGATTET into Smeerenburg fjord we find ourselves in surroundings devoured by ice and snow and completely devoid of every scrap of civilization, a place so barren and desolate that it is almost impossible to imagine that this very area once was the setting for a large-scale enterprise involving thousands of actors: the merciless, very profitable hunting of whales and walruses.

We pass Amsterdamøya, where the Dutch settlement Smeerenburg - Blubbertown - was one of the lively centers of the seasonal 17th century industry. Long since the echoing calls of busy men have silenced, the grim smell of slowly decaying carcasses has vanished. It was a risky job, and give - and - take; all around Spitsbergen, as we walk the shores and peninsulas, we find the shallow wooden-framed graves of those unfortunate whalers who died in accidents or from scurvy far away from home. Not even the earth welcomed them. Resting on the cold chest of the permafrost they had to be hidden under piles of stone, apart from which the most obvious trace of the era is a tragic one: the absence of the great whales in these waters.

Other adventurous human enterprises, though of a more noble kind, were later executed here. Through its accessibility and advanced northerly position Svalbard, around the turn of the century, was seen as a suitable starting ramp for assaults on the North Pole. All of these created a tremendous interest in the West, and journalists and spectators invaded the cold and remote scene of the archipelago. From Virgohamna, a stage of a natural amphitheater on Danish Island, the Swedish balloonist Andrée and his two companions set off on a fatal expedition in 1897, a spectacular show sponsored by the King and fired by strong beliefs in new technology and as strong nationalistic feelings. The slowly leaking balloon carried the men into the domains of the pack ice for only 58 hours before it was iced down. Over the ice the party struggled their way south and reached Kvitøya (White Island), where they weeks later all succumbed, maybe to trichinosis from Polar bear meat. Their remains where found by a sealer 33 years later, including their diaries – and their films, which amazingly could be developed!

Using a dirigible that evidently refused to share his heroic ideas, the American journalist Wellman made three consecutive attempts from Virgohamna to conquer the Polar ice sheet. None of them carried him more than a couple of miles, and he turned his interest to conquering the Atlantic instead. But the dreams about flying over the Pole persisted, and technology made steps forward. Still it wasn't until almost twenty years later, in 1926, that the daring men in their flying machines made it. Leaving from Ny Ålesund on Spitsbergen, the American admiral Byrd in his small, single prop machine, was the first to make a turn over the Pole. In Ny Ålesund he had already encountered the Norwegian explorer Roald Amundsen, the first to raise the flag on the South Pole, who together with the Italian engineer Nobile and their American sponsor Ellsworth, was preparing for an adventurous flight in an improved dirigible. They were the first to successfully cross the Polar ice and land in Alaska. An attempt by Nobile and an all-Italian crew to repeat the flight two years later failed. Heading on a rescue mission for his friend, Amundsen and his aeroplane was lost, never to be found. With that the starting ramp for the Pole was closed in Svalbard. But these flights all nourished the growing interest in the Arctic regions.

KONGSFJORDEN

WE HAVE SHAPED our course into Kongsfjorden, King's Bay, one of the loveliest fjords in Spitsbergen. The bottom of the fjord is reigned by the mighty King's glacier, pierced through by the aligned Three Crowns mountain peaks. The setting is backdropped by the Queens Range, covering its 3800 feet summit in an eternal cloak of snow. It is all majestic, and aptly christened in true Norse reverence for the Royal. All along the southern shore a narrow coastal plain stretches, broadening to a mile or so at its widest. Right at this spot a minor settlement of brightly colored wooden houses clings to the ground like a cluster of limpets on a skerry. Ny Ålesund, at 78° 55' N, is a former coal-mining settlement that boasts of as series of "northernmost in the world" features – like the shop, the art gallery, the small museum and the North Pole Hotel. Following a couple of explosions the mine was closed in 1961, and the settlement was later turned into a research center, where a broad spectrum of Arctic studies are undertaken. Adaptations to the severe climate by plants and animals are natural research objects as are glaciology and ecology. Vital for our understanding of the present and our planning for the future is research on other aspects of our predicament: airborne pollution, global warming and sea level rise, the depletion of the ozone layer... Though an international mix of about a hundred scientists are busy here during the summer, their activities do not discourage wildlife. Here the slender Arctic tern defends her nest by attacking the wanderer on his way to the northernmost post office in the world. Here the barnacle geese graze and nest between the houses, attracting the Arctic fox on raids for a winter store of eggs. At the roadside the red phalarope male is pinned to his nest in a camouflaging turf of grass. In the outskirts of town, the freshwater pond, set like a mirror in a frame of greenest moss, houses redthroated loons and long-tailed ducks. The birds share their swimming pool with the wild Svalbard reindeer, which there finds its drinking well. It is here in Ny Ålesund that we are most likely to meet these herbivores at close range.

In the early morning sun we see two of them - square, small silhouettes - ruminating the light veils of fog rising by the pond shore. Their heavy antlers, still in velvet, are the only impressive thing about them. Everything else is short, rendering them a compact look. Short legs, neck and snout all help to prevent heat loss and preserve energy. A long while we watch them slowly grazing their way along the moss-bank – nibbling lips, cutting teeth, grinding jaws, constantly chewing. Feeding on the low-growing vegetation, sand and pebbles are mixed in their diet, wearing down their teeth. Older reindeer die from starvation – often with a full stomach – since they simply cannot digest their poorly chewed sustenance. Having no predators, though the Polar bear is known to make rare attacks on sick or sleeping animals, they have developed sedentary, energy saving habits. Maybe this is why they – in spite of facing the toughest conditions of any sub-species - have the longest life-span of them all, reaching an age of 12-15 years. To obtain this they feed almost 24 hours a day throughout the summer, to build up a vital 40 – 60 pound layer of fat, which, in combination with a decrease or stop in body growth, will save the animals through the meager winter.

The Svalbard subspecies is exclusive to the area, and, surprisingly more closely related to the High Arctic Canadian caribou than to the wild reindeer of Scandinavia or Siberia. Thousands of years ago they must have migrated over the vast nowhere of the sea-ice from Greenland, an amazing feat! Apart from here in the beautiful Kings Bay, we at times from the deck see these long-way immigrants with great agility climb the steep, hazardous mountain slopes. And quite often we encounter them on our tundra walks, in the heart of the land they have made their home.

REINDYRS FLYA

REINDEER FLAT – a spontaneous decision on behalf of our expedition leader has brought us ashore on the largest expanse of tundra in Svalbard. At the beach the zodiacs rest inside some rocky outcrops, on which some brent geese have found a protected resting place. Apart from the coastal plains under the bird-cliffs, the tundra also supports a sparse plant life. To these oases, brackets in the deserts of rock and ice, all land-living life is confined. The tundra on its stretched out palm offers nesting sites for a number of birds, as well camouflaged as their eggs to fool the Arctic fox – if not strong enough to fend him off. Above all it is the most important ground for all the waders, and the home of the loon. No birds of prey disturb their hatching, though there are rare reports of the odd snowy owl sweeping over the tundra plain.

The tundra rolls away ahead to the horizon, shadows of clouds floating over the velvet ground, riding the gentle waves of continuous slopes. The rugged mountain peaks by the horizon give me a feeling of infinite time, the undulating tundra one of endless space. In this pristine land eternity is finally present. No trace of humans, no trees blocking my view, immense silence, soft wind stirring the pale-yellow petals of the poppy – the tundra and I breathe calmly. All of a sudden, from under some boulders clad in patches of orange and yellow lichens, there is a soft call "teeu-teuu": the little snow-bunting swings up, bursting out in a lark-like warble! A group of reindeer graze over there, only a handful – as many as will ever herd together in a land only 13 per cent biologically productive. Proceeding gently along, I find myself not pushing through the shrubs of the Arctic willow, but actually walking on their mouse-ear sized leaves!

I sit on a boulder once laid down by the retreating ice, with an unlimited view of melt-water ponds mirroring the sky where the permanently frozen ground retains the water – sapphires set in velvet mute shades of green and brown. At my feet lies the bleached antler of a reindeer, around it shine the purple faces of the saxifrage, mixed in with the white ones of the Mountain Aven, crouching away from the wind. The plants invite me down on my knees for a closer examination, constant reminders of the sturdy strength of life under the most extreme conditions.

Coming back, some 1000 feet from the shore we find a mysterious little hump abruptly rising from the boggy plain. To one side it is prolonged by two faint, slightly curved ridges, running like whispers under the moss. Even through the vegetation we can make out the grayish white, porous bone: a skull of a huge whale, preserved in the Arctic store house! In the shallow waters around Reindyrs-flya a Bowhead whale went for its final rest, maybe thousands of years ago. Our find indicates an old shore line and the still continuing rebounding of the land mass, so long pressed down by the enormous ice sheet.

On the shore we rest a while on silver-gray drift logs, carried here by currents and waves from Russian rivers, as far away as the troubled civilization. Snow starts drifting in from the sea. It is time to return to the comforting warmth of the ship. Comforting also is the thought that more than half of the wilderness areas in Svalbard are set aside as national parks, nature reserves and bird sanctuaries. Here human interferences such as industrial intervention, dumping of refuse and hunting are prohibited.

THE HANGING GARDEN

$$\text{———} \bullet \text{———}$$

THE SEA IS SMOOTH again as we slowly glide through ice filled waters. Among the chunks of ice, clouds hover, smiling to their reflected images, the color of the sky deepened in the water – the sea more sky than the sky itself. A skua is violently harassing a kittiwake out there, forcing it to throw up its meal, catching it in mid-air. Shaken, but alive and well, the victim heads for the bird cliff which also is our appointed goal. Or rather, we aim at the luxuriously rich garden that fringes its foot like a dropped, loosely folded dress in brilliant green.

Yes, there are places in Svalbard much richer in plant life than the waterlogged, rolling tundra. On this narrow coastal shelf the grass is higher, the flowers taller and more abundant than in any place we have seen as yet. Literally put in brackets, to one side by a glacier, to the other by steep rocks, reindeer are fenced out from the pasture, and it remains ungrazed. We find some 17 species in bloom, a third of them of the rich Saxifrage family. Among them is the sturdy purple one, the ultimate challenger of winds and snow, which has gained a grip as far as land extends in the High Arctic. It bundles up in low clusters to trap insulating air and to benefit from the warmer, more sheltered, micro-climate close to the ground. There snow-abrasion and desiccation from winds are reduced, and even a limited snowfall can fur the stunted plants from the bitter cold of the winter. The moss campion abides by these rules. Kneeling by one of the fluorescent green cushions with scattered pinkish stars is our botanist Sue Fenton, surrounded by a group of interested listeners. Sue's pants for certain have the hallmark of a plant-lover: wet and dirty knees!

Surrounded by the constant braying from the nesting birds we walk up to two rocks breaking through the lush carpet of grass and mosses. They face us under big, colorful wigs of plants, which even have gained a foot-hold in the crevices that scar the rock-face. It is a lovely sight: Chickweeds, Dandelion and Cinquefoil splashing the gray mineral in light, living colors. As we take a last step up to the rock for a closer inspection, the grinding background noise from the birds is abruptly cut off. In the sound-shadow the wee dripping of precious melt-water drops tickles our ears: melt-water enriched by guano from the birds above, melt-water that turns the primitive soil on the sterile rock into a flower-bed.

All together the flora of Svalbard is varied beyond comparison in the farthest north: some 160 flowering plants challenge the conditions here, while the neighboring Russian islands of Frans Josef Land support a mere 40. Apart from the Gulf stream warming west Svalbard, the reason for the abundance may be that parts of the archipelago were exempt from the lethal ice sheet of the last glaciation. From small glacial refuges a haphazard dispersal of plants recolonized the islands, much in the way they originally once got to this remote and isolated archipelago: bouncing and dancing along during periods of extensive sea-ice, most seeds and fruits were wind-swept here, covering amazing distances. Others were brought here by waves and currents, or hooked to feathers and hidden in the stomachs of migrating birds. In these desolate surroundings the flowers are such strong reminders of the wonder of adaptation. Already when the spring is yawning, they switch on their low-light metabolism, resuming life even under the thinning snow-cover. Not daring to rely on the few insects, the plants have a high level of self-fertility. In fact, most have a choice between sexual and asexual reproduction, in addition to being perennial, to secure survival.

Leaning down for a closer look at some tall Hawkweed-leaved saxifrages, a warm, earthy smell reaches us from the mosses. To the left, a couple of Arctic Buttercups stretch their tiny yellow bowls towards us. Be it in this hanging garden or on a walk over the tundra – to many of us the flowers shine brighter here, on the edge of the imaginable, than anywhere else.

ODOBENUS ROSMARUS – THE TOOTH-WALKER

JUST NORTH OF THE 80th degree, Moffen, a peculiar sand and gravel island resembling a low atoll, with some effort heaves itself out of the sea. Being a preferred site for walruses that haul out to rest, it in 1983 shared the status of protection given in 1952 to those puzzling animals. In old Norse they were called "whale-horses", and the whalers believed them to be a cross between an oxen and a whale. Females and males alike were hunted for their tusks, the ivory of Medieval Europe, and later persecuted for the oil. Russian hunters when they hunted them in the pack-ice used the up to two inches thick hide to protect the hull of their boats from the impact of the ice, but commercially more important was the use of it as drive-belts in the growing industry of Europe. A most useful animal, the Svalbard population almost shared the fate of the whales: 37 animals were seen during the entire 1960's.

The shallow waters around Moffen house banks of their favorite prey, clams and mussels. They locate these creatures at depths up to 260 feet with their stiff, short bristles, root them up with their snout, and in a lethal kiss, suck the mollusks out with their powerful lips – some 90 pounds a day to satisfy a 2400 pound adult male.

In the wee hours of a memorable Sunday morning outside Moffen, the cinnamon-colored, major lump of a resting male on the edge of an ice-floe attracted the zodiacs. A lead of open water paved the way between huge ice floes to the sleeping giant. Evidently he had not been in the balmy air very long; if so, he would have blushed, his blood being flushed to the surface of his hide to cool him. His 15-inch tusks were gleaming, heavy snores vibrated the wings of his nostrils, and the thick warmth of his body odor soon enveloped us. Concentrating on keeping the distance, we all too late noticed that a huge ice floe from behind was pushing us right on to the walrus. Stefan in the nearest zodiac desperately tried to paddle backwards, but in vain: the bow pushed against the animal. Forced out of his sleep, the walrus in an instant reared up, swaying his body to and fro, firing threatening glances out of the corner of his eye down at the frightened intruder. Under the belly of the beast, Stefan for a second feared that he would get crushed and the zodiac punctured. To everybody's surprise and relief the enormous heap of blubber rolled over sideways and splashed into the water. The incident gave the best close-up pictures you could wish for.

Walruses are renowned for being social, harmless creatures. The females have very deep motherly instincts, devotedly looking after their calf during a protracted period of parental care and 18 months of lactation. On land almost comically clumsy, they in their true element are turned into strong and swift swimmers. During courtship the males are agile dancers, adding to their ballet skills a drumlike song with an individual beat. It ends in a sharp, clean, ringing sound like that of a Tibetan gong to attract the females before they mate in the water. They undertake long migrations, about which we still have more to learn. Late satellite-tracking has shown individual trips from Edgeøya in the Southeast by Kveitøya in the Northeast all the way to Frans Josef Land and back in just a fortnight's time. This may well be the reason for the increase to an estimated 1000 animals on Svalbard over the last decades: the inaccessibility of those Russian islands once saved its population from becoming extinct, and now they "spill over" to Svalbard.

One fine morning in 1991 we spotted a group of them on a floe. The close encounter made it possible for our hawk-eyed naturalist Jack Swenson to make a lucky observation. Scrutinizing the photos taken that morning, Jack found a minute colored tag on the flipper of one of the animals. Forwarding his find to a team of Danish researchers on Greenland, their gratefulness knew no limits: this was the first evidence ever of migrations between the small east-Greenland population and that in Svalbard – Frans Josef Land, maybe indicating that they all belong to the same population.

Odobenade translates "toothwalker". The tusks are used to haul out on ice as well as to lean on when sleeping, but there is no evidence for the old belief that they are used to dig molluscs out with.

BIRDS, BIRDS, BIRDS – BY THE MILLION

THE HALLMARK OF the high Arctic nesting grounds is huge populations of a very limited number of species. As the light of the spring dawn slowly penetrates the four months of Polar darkness, millions of migrating seabirds invade their traditional nesting areas, well established since hundreds of years, and promptly noted in the logs of Barents' navigation: "...where there was so great a number of birds that they flew against our sails."* All birds have their defined niches, according to their need and capabilities: the islets and beaches, the tundra and the bird cliffs all support the miracle of life once ice and snow have loosened their grip in late spring or early summer.

As we passed the island of Birdsong, the northernmost outpost of west Spitsbergen, little auks** hung around the slopes like clouds, wheeling in and out as one body of birds in synchronized movement. Bands of the plump little bird broke out, bustling low over their reflected images on the smooth water, decisively heading for their fishing grounds. They and their feathered cousins are the living links between the plankton and algae bloom of the water and the vegetation of the barren land. Thus 100 000 little auks are estimated to bring in 70 tons of plankton in their throat pouches a month to feed their nestlings! The rich guano under the bird cliffs is what makes the primitive soils flourish, and so the birds spin the circle of energy flow between the elements: from water through air to soil – some of it seeping back to the sea with rain and melt-water flow!

Heading along the north coast among ice floes in lovely sunshine. To the North the sea mirrors an open sky in a mild and rich yellow, crisscrossed by bands of guillemots flying in all directions. The land to the South rests under a blackish overcast sky and dense banks of fog. A couple of puffins etch long lines swimming in the smooth water. We turn south into Hinlopen strait, between Spitsbergen and the island of Nordaustlandet. The scenery has slowly changed, the high peaked mountains are replaced by lower, far stretching plateaus divided by deep valleys. It is more desert-like and the air is colder, but the water is open enough for us to proceed. Birds are increasing in the air as we approach one of the most spectacular cliffs in Svalbard, Alkefjellet. The frowning cliff is an astounding geological feature. Like the worn and torn pipes of a giant's organ or the deteriorating spires and towers of a medieval cathedral, the pillars of dolomite rise straight up some 300 feet from the sea, every ledge and platform crowded to its edge with Brunnich guillemots! Amazingly, before they can fly properly the chicks will make their perilous leaps from these heights.

The breeze carries to us the grating, growling "arr-arr" from the guillemot choir mixed with whiffs of an old chicken farm and an abandoned fish shop. In front of us is a wonderful scene, full of everyday guillemot life, tuxedoed birds energetically flapping in precipitate flight, birds missing their landings, neighborly quarrels on the ledges, and on the water they skim and paddle away as we pass. To imagine these birds out there in open leads and cracks in the ice during the Polar night! Pretty small and fragile by appearance, they must be among the sturdiest creatures in the world. On the ledges, their black backs turned to the sea, they incubate the one egg precariously laid right on the narrow shelves. Wisely it is pear-shaped – bumps and winds swing it around its own axis rather than roll it over the edge. And right there and then, from the bow of the ship, we can meditate on the wonder of life, as the nestlings are fed with fish: fins transformed to wings, scales to feathers, lips to beaks in the eternal flow and transition of energy.

* G. de Veer: Three voyages by the Northeast, Amsterdam 1598
** In American dove-kies

The Brunnich guillemots have been recorded to dive some 300 feet in pursuit of fish. The tuxedoed birds in their erect posture remind you about their southern counterparts and non-relatives, but contrary to the penguins they can fly.

NORDAUSTLANDET

UNDER AN OVERCAST SKY cut open by widening sleets we weave our way between good-sized ice floes on a south-easterly course, deeper into the Hinlopen straight. As more light penetrates the cloud cover, a dim rainbow emanating from the light fog arches over the ship and moves along with us, a constant gate to the magic land emerging at the horizon.

Not always is it possible to proceed very far into these waters; this is the ice-bound eastern side, largely affected by cold Polar water flowing into the Barents Sea from the North. Warm summers crack up the ice, and fairly open water invites us to explore the coast of Nordaustlandet, the second-largest and most heavily glaciated island in the archipelago. We pass Vibebukta, where the coast still is locked by land-fast sea ice, dotted with the scattered bodies of ringed seals. This is a sight far more exciting to us than the peaceful picture might suggest: here are the hunting-grounds of the Lord of the Arctic. A tingle of energy stirs our senses.

Ahead the land offers us a totally new face as the low silvery line floating by the horizon keeps growing while we sneek up to it between icebergs and floes. This is a natural phenomenon seen in few places of the world: a majestic wall, an up to a good 100 feet high ice front, protruding to the coast for 125 undefiled miles of purest white and blue. Nowhere is the integrity and inhospitality of the land more obvious than here, nowhere is the beauty of the ice more awe-inspiring. Austfonna, an ice cap more than 1800 feet thick, in places extends into this floating shelf, from where fair-sized icebergs, several hundred feet long break out to cruise the sea. As we close in on the glistening front, we are breathtaken by another feature: melt-water cascading down the ice cliff, spouting over its edge in a series of powerful falls sectioning the entire width of the endless wall!

– Unearthly, says the lady passenger beside me.

As the hour grows late, passengers reluctantly retreat for some rest, their PA-system set on Channel one for a hoped-for wake up call. The cloudcover has been swept away, visibility is excellent. For us naturalists it is hard to give in to the need for rest. We don't want to miss anything that might appear among the golden bergs and floes, where the odd bearded seal hauls out and basks in the warmth of the light. The soft murmur of the rippling water around the bow is broken by an occasional, powerful "phoouu" as a walrus blows out there. Standing erect, shoulders high over the surface, one of them in a prolonged glance watches Polaris slowly passing. As much as we enjoy and appreciate the encounter, he is not what we are looking for…

The hunt is on, the fever is there. Fuelled through the light night by high expectations, we welcome our bartender Bob, who pops up at the right moment to thaw us with hot chocolate or Irish coffee as we take turns at the scope. Chances are … And all of a sudden!

– There, on that ice floe at two o'clock! Look, look!

– No, I don't really think …

– But yes, the yellowish hump there…

– No, no, I'm pretty sure it is dirty ice. Algae…

– It looked like fur to me!

Even mistakes fire our hopes and renew our energy. For a long while our conversation lingers on the "white fur", the big game for our weapon-less hunt. Until we actually have spotted him, his name is taboo. Thus we share the original inuit hunters deep respect for the mystery and power of the animal.

THE WHITE FUR

━━━◆━━━

WHEN THE ICE RETREATS in the summer, parts of the White fur population goes ashore to a lean season in most areas of the Arctic, feeding on eggs, berries and seaweed. In some areas they even graze the grassy meadows, or sleep the meager months away. In West Svalbard we see them in the fjords and on islands at times. But their natural habitat coincides with the ringed seals' realm in the ice – the only place they can catch this preferred prey. Thus they have developed into non-territorial roamers, covering long distances during the summer, following the retreating ice edge into the colder eastern part of Svalbard. Here they remain active hunters in the ice, and here – as opposed to most parts of the Arctic – we stand a good chance of seeing them in their true surroundings. Perfectly adapted to the seasonal changes of their hunting grounds, they bridge two differing categories: hunting in the pack-ice makes them, in a sense, true marine mammals, but they are also the largest land-living carnivore on earth today.

The golden midnight light has slowly turned red. It is reflected on the faces of my fellow hunters, giving them a tanned and healthy look in spite of a growing weariness. Certainly – the sea and the ice reward only patience! An encounter with the White fur cannot be guaranteed. We have been lucky over the years, but right now our alertness is somewhat dulled, our hopes low. But at three-thirty in the morning Bud Lenhausen, with a triumphant smile, jumps back from the scope: – Swimming polar bear right ahead!

Still too small to be clearly descerned through binoculars, the scope reveals the pointed, triangular shape of a fairly small head on a stretched out, prolonged neck. The V-shaped wake around the animal also tells us that this is no seal. Immediately Captain Kent slows down the ship, and so as not to stress the bear, we cautiously diverge from his course. Renowned to be a swimmer of fabulous stamina, it still is a strange sight to see him – or her*

– in icy waters some 15 miles from the nearest coast. He is floating quite high, the thick, insulating blubber and the air-filled hairs of his fur adding to his buoyancy.

The announcement has already been made, and people silently gather along the rails just in time to see him, with a powerful jerk, throw himself up on a floe. Water flushes from him. He is a magnificent sight, and very much aware of our presence. For a while he freezes his step, one large, furred paw in midair while he slowly turns his head to check us. Then he shakes the water off his oily coat, dog-like. Making no haste, he lumbers off across the ice. Now and then he stops, half turning, sniffing the air, relying on his extraordinarily keen sense of smell to identify what we are.

In a sudden movement he rolls over in the dry snow, which acts like blotting-paper, and when he deflates himself into a restful pose, the chin comfortably resting on crossed front paws, the fur is dry. To our eyes, he seems to be a healthy sub-adult, well-fed and rounded in appearance, probably between three and four years old. If we are right, he is obviously a successful youngster, who not too long ago parted from his mother to execute his learned skills in stalking and still-hunting seals – their two main hunting methods. Most common on the æstival ice is still-hunting, which, like stalking, demands extreme patience and concentration. The bear may stand or lie absolutely motionless for hours on end by the ringed seals' breathing holes, waiting to kill and fling it up on the ice in one single stroke by the powerful paw with sharp, finger-long claws. Since ringed seals are wonders of nervous alertness, most killing attempts are unsuccessful, even for an experienced adult bear. The overall conditions in Svalbard are so harsh, that only an estimated 30 % of the cubs are likely to reach sexual maturity. Starvation is the most common cause of death during the first two years after the youngsters have been abandoned by their mother.

---

* It is almost impossible to seperate young males and females by sight only. It could as well be a she-bear.

THE ICE BEAR

IT IS SAID THAT the Polar bear is the loneliest animal on earth. In most parts of the Arctic they roam the ice in solitude, males avoiding each other and females bonding only their cubs. Bears have been seen at the Pole of Inaccessibility, 86° N, as well as close to the North Pole, in the middle of the sterile ice desert. These lonely roamers are exceptions. Tagged bears have been tracked from Svalbard to Greenland, but many bears are confined to a home area, their northern range being limited to 82° N where nutrient-rich water fades out into the deep Polar basin and seals are no longer available.

Only during some time in April and May when they mate, do males and females share life in the shifting ice. Then they part, and from this moment on a wonderful series of adaptations is revealed in the saga of bear reproduction. Though fertilized, her eggs remain dormant in a postponed implantation, a strategy of survival that gives her a chance to hunt undisturbed for four months to build up a 400 pound layer of blubber. This blubber is her cupboard when in late October she withdraws to a snow den. By then the dormant eggs have started their growth. Inside the womb, the fetuses develop on nourishment drawn from the mother's blood, a process that weakens her immensely and may be lethal were it to continue. The average two cubs are given an early birth to in late December – one pound and a half of blind, deaf and nearly naked life – in the sheltered darkness of the den. Again, behind this startling premature birth of mini-cubs lies a sensible strategy of survival. After birth, the cubs are breast-fed with milk containing 31% butter fat produced from her built-up layer of blubber, a more survivable solution. When in March she breaks the seal of the den to introduce the world to her 25 pound cubs, their main prey, the ringed seals, have just given birth to their pups and are abundant. By then the mother bear might be lean after a six to seven months' fast, but she is fully capable of leading her off-spring through their first steps on the path to self-supporting individuals. Constantly caressing and correcting them with low throat sounds, she will care for them over the next two years or more with an affection so deep that she will sooner die than desert them.

To the native people of the Arctic, the Polar bear was a magic animal held in reverence and often worshipped. By many tribes he was even considered their forefather. Nevertheless he was hunted, every single part of the animal being useful. The bear was often asked to forgive his hunter: "Pardon us now, forget that we have killed you." After the killing the bear was usually propriated with a great feast. This all reflects that "any society that lives by hunting spends most of its time thinking about the animals that it hunts."* And it is a very far cry from the commercial hunting that, following the opening of the North, drove many animal populations to the edge of extinction. The efficiency of the skilled Norwegian hunters with their "self-kill" set gun, today makes horrifying reading. In the 1920s and 30s the Bear King, Henri Rudy, alone killed about 800 bears. Growing safari hunting from the beginning of the 1950s increased the annual kill to 300 bears for two decades, shackling the Svalbard population with a lethal pressure.

In 1973 a five-nation agreement gave circumpolar protection to the Polar bear. This agreement allows a quota for Inuits, Eskimos, but apart from that bears can only be killed in self-defense. This has lead to a welcome increase in the Svalbard population. Sadly, new threats have emerged, the consequences of which are still unknown. Pollution of the seas has brought PCB, a toxic chemical compound which does not break down and which accumulates through the food-chain, to concentrations that cause concern in the Svalbard population of Polar bears. This stresses the need to continue researching these majestic mammals, the Lords of the Arctic.

* E. Clark Howell, American anthropologist, 1965.

HUMAN IMPACT

THE ANCHOR RATTLES DOWN. We are back to where our Odyssey around Svalbard started. Surrounded by wild mountain peaks and two mighty glaciers to the bow, the Polaris in the majestic sunlit fjord of Hornsund certainly is a nimble little ship. We inhale the atmosphere of a smiling Arctic in deep breaths as we board the zodiacs and speed towards a shoaling landing where the outflow of tidal water makes conditions change all the time. First ashore is Craig Holt with the rifle – this is Polar bear country, and much better safe than sorry. As soon as the sound of the engines has died away we are totally enclasped with the shrill "kitti-waking" of thousands of voices, while the humming background sound of blurred guillemot calls cape the mountain in a dense acoustic carpet.

At the south end of the Sofiekammen mountain-range, Gnålodden is but a shelf of deposited debris embracing the foot of the towering bird cliff, but it welcomes us with an uncommonly lush carpet of mosses and grass, decorated with a richness of flowers. Close to the beach stands the small tarpaper-covered hut of the Norwegian trapper Odd Ivar Ruud. Since long abandoned it has been kept in decent shape by Polar bear researchers. A couple of plank beds, an iron stove and a table with chairs are squeezed into two tiny rooms. Cozy as it may look to us on an enchanting summer day, few of us would consider spending two weeks there in the Polar night, not to mention wintering! But, keeping up the traditions of Russian hunters, Ruud up to the 1970's hunted fox, goose, duck and Polar bear. The "self-kill", a set gun mounted to be triggered by the bear itself, is no longer at the hut. It was a widely used, lethal device which did not separate a female with cubs from a hungry male…

Only years after the discovery in 1596, the wildlife of Svalbard was recognized as an untouched, extremely rich resource by European companies.

Oil was in demand for soap-making, street-lighting and lubrication, and the initial smash-and-grab assaults on this no-man's land were aimed at the walrus and the whales. Having become unprofitable, the west European expeditions in the 18th century were exchanged for smaller ones by the Russian Pomors, a tribe of wintering hunters from the White Sea area. Their hunting-grounds, spread all over Svalbard, were gradually taken over by Norwegians in the 19th century. Initially – like the Pomors – some were sent out by trading companies, many of them later made it a self-chosen way of life. In contrast to the Pomors, who often hunted on an ecologically sound revolving system, the motto of these trappers, in the days when little was known about population-sizes, was: "Kill what you can today, or someone else will get it."

Some impact of the hunting:

Bowhead and right whales: Extinct in the area.

Walruses: Severely threatened. Protected in 1952. Originally tens of thousands, there are today maybe a thousand. Recovering.

Polar bears: Threatened by new efficient hunting methods and safari hunters. Protected world-wide in 1973. Increasing.

Eider ducks: Severely depleted since down and eggs, as well as the ducks themselves, were collected. Protected in 1953.

Reindeer: In 1925 a couple of hundred were left of an estimated original 10.000. In that year Norway got the sovereignty over Svalbard, and the reindeer was immediately protected. Seems to have regained its optimum.

Walking back to the zodiacs and a wet departure from Gnålodden, we see a huge congregation of trumpeting Barnacle geese by the shore. This lovely bird, speckled in black and white, was also threatened. Today we enjoy an increase of this protected species.

IN THE INTEREST OF FUTURE GENERATIONS

NOT LONG AGO man came to Svalbard from afar, to penetrate the cold waters and coasts in a relentless search for profit. A mere 400 years of human involvement left heavy marks of impact on the populations of mammals and birds in Svalbard. The original food-chains, developed and maintained over thousands of years, were disrupted and many of the species were driven to the edge of extinction. Once man began taking interest in minerals, arising conflicts between companies of different nationalities could only be solved by depriving the archipelago of its status of a no-man's land. The Treaty that in 1925 handed the sovereignty of the area to Norway, in its second Article, pinpoints the new owner's duty to "enforce... regulations to secure the preservation and – if necessary – the re-establishment of animal and plant life within the areas mentioned and their territorial waters."

The last few decades have seen tremendous progress as species after species has won protection in an attempt to reestablish the original populations. In 1973 their major habitats were turned into national parks, reserves or sanctuaries. More than half of the archipelago was given a chance to regain its former splendor. With the exception of the baleen whales, the recovery of the animal populations has been successful. Most of the land is closed to future exploitation of minerals and exploratory drilling for oil has so far proved wasted.

There are other threats though. We know that all life in Svalbard is linked to and totally dependent upon the sea. The cod, herring and capelin have all experienced over-fishing, and the hope of finding oil in the shallow, ice-infested Barents Sea basin has recently supported hazardous drilling in a very sensitive area. But it is necessary to recognize, beyond short-sighted profits, the unique values of a resource that is rapidly disappearing – wilderness areas not tamed by man, which have original qualities and where ecosystems are not totally altered. Svalbard today again certainly has these characteristics.

The fleet of zodiacs floats in the evening sun. Leaving the shore after a late tundra visit we experience something rare: A minkie whale takes interest in our inflatables. In silence we spend 15 minutes wishing it to the surface near us to blow. Right beside us, unexpectedly at uneven intervals she emerges, revealing her curiosity, feeding our own. Moments like these make our appreciation of the rough, outdoor comfort of the rubber-boats grow. To the operations of the Polaris they are, in many ways, what the kayaks were to the traditional Inuits, taking us to our hunting grounds of experience and revelation. Their agile and swift maneuvers bring us close to the very wilderness heart of Svalbard.

Coming close to a wilderness area of such integrity and beauty puts our life in perspective. It evokes feelings that provoke rethinking. The frowning glaciers and the peaked mountains seem to restore the balance between man and nature, lost since Eden; here I, a man, am so small and the eternal strength of the natural processes so evident. One feels humble facing the sturdiness of life, manifest in the adaptation to these High Arctic surroundings by the Chickweed as well as the Polar bear or the pinhead-sized spider climbing the branches of his moss forest. They all tell you that life is rich, precious – and, as we know, vulnerable.

One morning in early August we found the following passenger message on the "Lost and Found" list aboard the Polaris:

"Lost: myself somewhere among the gliding icebergs and the popping brash ice of Hornsund, or with the swirling guillemots and gulls of Bear Island. If found, please do not return until August 14th."

As well as any, these words reflect a personal need that most of us share – to lose ourselves and through moments of peace of mind find a new perspective on our everyday lives in the struggling civilization. Few places offer us that possibility the way Svalbard does.

"OFF SEASON" SVALBARD

—◆●◆—

A THUD AWAKES ME and I roll over in the berth to look for the source of this unexpected noise in the wilderness. I notice that one of the shutters blinds off the bright light pouring through the window of the old hut, and I can tell Stefan and our friend Mats to go on sleeping. I hear no wind but evidently there is some, moving over the vast expanses of fast sea-ice outside, strong enough to swing the shutter on its frozen hinges. In my resumed sleep I feel a presence, a worry awakes me to new viligance. Through the window I stare straight into the pitch-black eyes of a fully grown Polar bear. His head fills the complete frame of the window.

- He is here, the bear is on visit!

I fling myself out of bed and reach for the gun. Stefan and Mats have extracted themselves from their cocoons of sleep. Where is the camera?! Excited as we are, we still are aware of the danger. Polar bears have quite often made their way through plank walls, so it is not much of a comforting thought that the window seems too small to let him in. The goings-on inside are enough to make the bear slowly retreat down the slope of snow that the wind has swept up against the wall. Forty feet away he stops and gazes at our faces, now in the open window. When he lowers his head in a manner we know might indicate an attack, Mats in response fires a detonating cap. The bear swings around, gallops a short distance and then falls back into a slow, steady lumbering. In the freezing cold air we remain in the open door to see him vanish among the ice ridges, into the frozen realms of his Kingdom.

This is the third morning of our visit to Svalbard. During two weeks in April 1994 Stefan and I, lead by our friend Mats Forsberg, experienced our favorite area "off season."Or, anyway, in another season than the Arctic summer. We covered some 600 miles of untouched snow on scooters, deep into the inland valleys, ascending on to the backs of glaciers, descending again to roam the sea-ice of the west and east coasts.

Nothing irregular breaks the coating of softly undulating snow covering the mountainous landscape. The air is crystal clear under an overcast sky. The wind chill factor adds dramatically to the cold as we drive at good speed through the night. We make stops to inhale the deep silence and check the area, gratefully acknowledging the efficiency of our face masks, which make us look like bank robbers but certainly save us from frost bite.

As we approach our temporary home the sky clears. To our surprise we see that the sea ice has started breaking up. We watch as a widening blue smile splits the white sheet just a mile from the shore. To the West the sun breaks out of the cloud cover, ascending towards the horizon - to suddenly stop and start rolling sideways, a wheel of fire! From our scooters, on the sea ice in - 4 F (- 20 C), we witness the magic happening – from now on the sun will dance above the horizon for the next four months! It is April 9, the first night of midnight sun. From some frozen-in ice sculptures we hear the broken barking of an Arctic fox. Suddenly he darts out of his hide-out and approaches us, curiosity defeating fear. Only 20 feet away he stops, and in an instant has swirled around, a white flash crossing the bluish, wind-patterned snow. Following him through our binoculars we catch a glimpse of a Polar bear. Behind her leap roll and stumble two soft balls of fur! Maybe this magic night offers her cubs their first hunting experience after leaving the den as they scout the ice edge out there. The voices of guillemots and kittiwakes reach us. The quiet air, where earlier only fulmars soared soundlessly, is all of a sudden filled with the sounds of Spring! Not surprisingly, this is the time of the year that the people in Svalbard welcome the most. And for Stefan and me it is only a matter of weeks until we return here, to share the impressions of the teeming life in this Arctic cathedral of Nature with the passengers of the Polaris.

SOME FACTS ABOUT SVALBARD

O VER THE MILLENNIA since the last glaciation of the North, Svalbard remained uninhabited by man. Wildlife was thriving in undisturbed balance, following the annual rhythm of the expanding and retreating ice sheet. Linked to the teeming but varying productivity of the sea, the wildlife has always been submitted to natural fluctuations. And, as we have learned, it encountered man. Today we find five species of seals – the bearded, the harp, the hooded, the ringed and the harbor seals – predated by the Polar bear and the Arctic fox. Walruses are increasing, reindeer plentiful. At sea to the South leaps the white-beaked dolphin, to the North the narwhale makes occasional visits. In the coastal waters the blows of the minkies and the white whale are mixed with the calls of millions of sea birds. These four species comprise 95% of the birds – the Brunnich guillemot, the fulmar, the little aulk and the kittiwake. But no fewer than 163 species have been recorded in the area – just about one species for every flowering plant! Most are stray visitors, 30 nest, and only the ptarmigan winters.

The whalers raided the Svalbard waters for about a century from 1610, but never wintered. The Pomors, coming from the White Sea area with a tradition of surviving under Arctic conditions were the first to winter there. Norwegian hunters first arrived in Pomor joint expeditions, but soon replaced them completely. The first part of the19th century saw few expeditions, but 1895-1941 an average of 25 hunters wintered each year. Today five resident trappers try to survive, mainly on the Arctic fox.

During the 19th century a growing number of scientists also found their way to the area, mapping and surveying it in ever-growing detail. They paved the way for an invasion that would imprint human permanence on a much larger scale; around the turn of the century, the minerals of Svalbard became of interest to man. A Klondike-fever brought different nationalities to make claims on gypsum, marble and, above all – coal. Growing competition in the no-man's land stressed the need of law and order. In the WW I peace negotiations in Paris, the Svalbard Treaty made the area part of Norway. In 1925 Longyearbyen, the biggest coal mine, was made the "capital," and the seat for the Governor, *Sysslomannen* in Norwegian.

When Russia signed the treaty and bought two former Dutch mines in the 30's, the multinational mix melted down to Russians and Norwegians. Both countries today continue the exploitation of coal in the Isfjorden area. The Russian settlements, Barentsburg and Pyramiden, house some 1800 people, while Longyearbyen houses about 1200. The small mining settlement of Svea, and the research center at Ny Ålesund today add some 70 residents. Like so many remote areas, Svalbard was not spared WW II. The British navy evacuated all inhabitants and set the mines in Longyearbyen and Barentsburg on fire in 1941. The Germans later destroyed the abandoned settlements, including Svea, and established a chain of weather stations in Svalbard. After the war everything was rebuilt, the mines repaired and mining further developed. The Russian mines are probably as non profitable as the Norwegian ones, which are heavily subsidized by the state. Doubtlessly strategic reasons have maintained human presence in the area.

What will the future of the archipelago be? Science and education are state supported alternatives to the mining, and there is of old an additional industry – tourism. In the roadless country it has traditionally been small-scale and shipborn, but today it is possible to take guided trekking or overland skiing tours, as well as to climb mountains and go snow-scootering. The tourism is nature and wildlife oriented and there is concern that its growth may have a negative impact. This growth is welcome though it requires our recognition of the responsibilities. To put half of the area aside as national parks and reserves in 1973 was only the first in a series of wise steps to regulate human presence and protect the beauty of the scenery and the vulnerable wildlife in harsh, lovely Svalbard.

The small mining settlement of Svea. Sweden started up the mining there in 1917, but sold the mine to Norway in 1934. The price was US $ 125 000.